21 Stories of Generosity

With CJ Hitz

21 Stories of Generosity
© 2013 Body and Soul Publishing

Published in the United States of America

ISBN-13: 978-0615923109
ISBN-10: 0615923100

Table of Contents

Introduction

By CJ Hitz

Generosity is a powerful word.

Webster's Dictionary defines it as "the quality of being kind, understanding, and not selfish; the quality of being generous; especially: willingness to give money and other valuable things to others."

Generosity can come in many forms including time, money, attention, service, or simply a kind word or compliment. Ultimately, the motive behind it is what's truly important.

Most of us could probably sit down and write a book when thinking of all the instances we've been on the giving or receiving end of generosity. Either way can be loads of fun...though Jesus did say, "It is more blessed to give than to receive." (Act 20:35)

Jesus knew a little something about generosity. "The proof is in the pudding," as they say. Generosity oozed out of every pore in Jesus' body. He gave sight to the blind, hearing to the deaf, attention to the outcast, cleansing to the leper, food for the hungry, and even new life to the dead.

And in one final Act of Generosity that trumps all others, he gave Himself completely in death so that mankind could be restored and freed from the curse of sin. As 1 Timothy 2:5-6 (NLT) proclaims...

"For there is only one God and one Mediator who can reconcile God and humanity—the man Christ Jesus. He gave his life to purchase freedom for everyone. This is the message God gave to the world at just the right time."

I'm so thankful for the Lord's extravagant generosity in my life and His grace that drew me to Himself in the spring of 1993.

In the 21 stories that follow, you're going to see unique snapshots of God's generosity as He uses people. Each one of us has the potential to be a powerful tool in the hands of God. May this little book give you inspiration as you enjoy seeing generosity through the eyes of each of the authors.

It's our prayer that you'll grow a little closer to the Author of generosity.

#1: The Barbie Blessing

By Darlene Shortridge

Jonna watched as my friend and her daughter recognized us and waved as they walked down our aisle in the grocery store. "Mama, I don't want to give my baby away."

My three year old daughter was sitting in the grocery cart staring at me with glossy eyes, fearful that I would make her give away her little Kelly doll she had gotten the day before for her birthday. "Sweetheart, you don't have to give your baby away. That was your birthday present." She was very perceptive for a three year old and knew that our friends were having a hard time financially. We weren't rich by any means but we tightly budgeted and did whatever it took to make ends meet.

We both watched as my friend pulled her cart alongside mine. Her one year old daughter scrutinized Jonna's baby while we talked. Jonna held the doll protectively against her chest while my friend and I discussed a few things. We said our goodbyes then we parted ways.

I smiled at my daughter. "See, you still have your baby. No one is going to take her away from you."

About half way through the store I heard her sweetly say, "I want to give her my baby doll."

While I encourage my children to give generously, I do not believe they have to give away everything they own. "Why do you want to give your baby away?"

"Well, she doesn't have a baby and Jesus wants me to."

How can you argue with that? I was proud of my daughter. She had a firm grasp of compassion and mercy at such a young age.

We went in search of our friends and when we found them, Jonna willingly handed over her baby with a smile.

Even though she did what she felt was right, I could still see the tears welling up in her eyes. I knew giving that baby away was a sacrifice for her and that God would reward her obedience. I tried to share with her the words of wisdom from Luke 6:38 which read: "Give, and it will be given to you. A good measure, pressed down, shaken together and running over, will be poured into your lap. For with the measure you use, it will be measured to you."

In terms she could understand I explained how God would bless her because of her obedience to him.
She nodded her little head but I could tell she still didn't quite understand how God could bless her. She was only three.

We arrived at home with a trunk full of groceries. As I pulled the first two sacks from the car, the lady next door came over. "Hey Darlene, does Jonna like Barbies?"

"Yeah, she loves them, why?"

"Well, my daughter has outgrown them and we have a huge box of stuff we don't want anymore. I thought Jonna might enjoy them,"

4

I couldn't help but grin. "She'd be thrilled."

I finished unloading the groceries and quickly put them away before I went to retrieve the box from our neighbor's house. Indeed, the box was huge and filled to the top with Barbies, clothes, cars, a house, a swimming pool, furniture, and so much more. I set the box down on the floor and started pulling the items out, one by one.

Jonna's eyes lit up as we examined each piece coming from the box. By the time we were done emptying the box, she had twenty-six Barbies and multiple accessories, too many to mention. We set up the pool on the deck and filled it with water. We played Barbies all afternoon.

Jonna learned an important lesson that day. She learned to give without expectation and she learned obedience is always better than sacrifice. God rewarded her in such an overwhelming way that it completely took her by surprise, all because she gave away one little doll.

I love sharing this message when I speak on giving because we can learn so much from this simple true story. I believe that Christ calls us to give without question and without expectation. He wants us to surrender all that we have into his capable hands and follow his instructions with all he has entrusted us with. Isn't everything his anyway?

What are you holding back today? What are you tightly holding on to? Give it to God and watch and see what he can do. Nothing is impossible with God!

Bio:
Darlene Shortridge is the best-selling author of Contemporary Christian Fiction. She coauthored "40 Day Publishing" with

her husband, Daniel. She lives in Oklahoma City. Connect with Darlene on most social media platforms. To contact Darlene about speaking at your next event, email her at darlene@darleneshortridge.com.

#2: Generosity of the Heart

By Laura J. Marshall

As the years pass and famine seems to cover the land, my acts of tangible generosity feel so limited. When I see the faces of children, pictures shared by friends or hearing of a neighbor taking their child out for a treat, part of my heart crumbles and falls at my feet. We've struggled and cut corners…stretching meals, using less electricity at night, turning off cable, and becoming a one car family. Extracurricular activities have become almost nonexistent.

Through this time, God has been teaching us about generosity, a generosity of spirit. The commodities I have to give now are my service, my time, my love. There are moments I've cried out to God, feeling I have nothing but the well of the spirit He has given me. There are moments when I feel as if I want to die if another person were to show me their generosity and I can't reciprocate. I feel bereft. I cry to Him and say, "Only from Your hand, Father. Don't make me have to accept the tangible when I have nothing to give back but with what I've come into the world."

I cried this and refused to speak of my lack, to Him or anyone. I was burdened and cast down. In His wisdom, He sent a friend. He sent others. People I didn't know with things only God knew our family needed, breakfast for our children, and a basket for Thanksgiving from our church miraculously appeared at our door.

Generosity has many forms. It can be in the constancy of a friendship, listening, time spent with another, and time spent in service for someone. In my brokenness, I have felt the lesson God has been giving me on generosity pour over my spirit. He doesn't see my lack. He sees the beauty that comes from a humble spirit and as I reach out with words or time or love, He shows me their worth. It's still hard to accept tangible generosity. He knows how much I long to lend and give and lavish on those I love and those less fortunate. However, He is teaching my family and I about the most important things in life and a generosity of the heart.

"Command those who are rich in this present world not to be arrogant nor to put their hope in wealth, which is so uncertain, but to put their hope in God, who richly provides us with everything for our enjoyment. Command them to do good, to be rich in good deeds, and to be generous and willing to share. In this way they will lay up treasure for themselves as a firm foundation for the coming age, so that they may take hold of the life that is truly life." - 1 Timothy 6:17-19

Bio:
Laura J. Marshall is a full-time mom of five boys. When not on active duty, she is the best-selling author of The Battle Cry Devotional series and inspirational fiction (historical romantic suspense, YA, and contemporary romance). She operates a popular blog called The Old Stone Wall which hosts and promotes Christian and clean books and encourages interaction between authors and readers. Visit Laura on Facebook or Twitter or visit her website at
http://www.LauraJMarshall.com

#3: Sacrificial Love: A Life of Generosity

By Krystal Kuehn

Self-sacrificing. Selfless. Generous. I thought I was being all this every time I gave away something I thought I needed and really liked, or when I gave my time to help someone out. I never imagined that you could live your entire life this way, every day, all the time. Well, that is precisely what I began to learn since my son was born several years ago.

I want to sit down and relax. He wants to play. I start making dinner, but he is hungry NOW. I want to go for a nice walk and get some fresh air, but he does not want to leave the house. I want to sleep in just a little more. He is up and ready to go.

I couldn't do what I wanted, when I wanted anymore! I never considered my "freedoms" as something to be appreciated until I had to give them up. One by one, in every area of my life, I learned about sacrificing my own well-being for someone else's. I learned about true generosity as well, and how giving without expecting anything in return can become a lifestyle.

I was fortunate enough to have the option of staying home with my son while he was growing up, but that also was not without sacrifice of other goals and dreams. Although they did not die, what did was self. I died to my own comforts, privileges, and pursuits.

I have since adjusted to the many changes in my life. And now I ponder on how much it has changed me as a person. I looked up the meaning of the word "sacrifice." According to the American Heritage Dictionary, it means to forfeit (one thing) for another thing considered of greater value; to sell or give away at a loss. A sacrifice costs you something – something that is valuable to you. But, you are willing to give it away because what you will gain is even greater and more important to you.

Isn't that just what Jesus did? He made the ultimate sacrifice. He gave up His position in heaven, became a servant here on earth, and ultimately gave His very life for you and me. The Bible says,

"Let this same attitude and purpose and (humble) mind be in you which was in Christ Jesus: (Let Him be your example in humility) Who, although being essentially one with God and in the form of God (possessing the fullness of the attributes which make God, God), did not think this equality with God was a thing to be eagerly grasped or retained. But stripped Himself (of all privileges and rightful dignity), so as to assume the guise of a servant (slave), in that He became like men and was born a human being. And after He appeared in human form, He abased and humbled Himself (still further) and carried His obedience to the extreme, even the death of the cross!" (Philippians 2:5-8, Amplified).

We are so precious and valuable to God that He was willing to sacrifice so much for our benefit!

I suppose we can assess how much the people in our lives mean to us by how much we are willing to sacrifice for them. I was always grateful and aware that my son was a blessing from God, but I never realized how much he meant to me until I gave up so much of myself for him. There were many occasions where I complained and felt frustrated and angry. But, I didn't realize that my losses would result in such great gain. Not only is it rewarding to see my son grow and have his many needs met, but I have grown as a parent. I have learned that sacrificial love can be a way of life.

With Jesus as our example, we can live each day solely to serve the Lord. And the way we serve the Lord is by serving others. What a difference daily sacrifices we make can have on our children, spouse, friends, and others! Sometimes we may never know. Yet, are we willing to humble ourselves and esteem their interests as being more important than our own?

May we never miss the many opportunities that come our way by counting them as nothing more than drudgery or insignificant or unappreciated. And, with every opportunity may we be reminded of God's love and His sacrifice to us because our lives will never be the same again!

Bio:
Krystal Kuehn, MA, LPC, LLP, NCC is a psychotherapist, best-selling author, teacher, musician and songwriter. Krystal specializes in helping people live their best life now, reach their full potential, overcome barriers, heal from their past, & develop a happiness lifestyle. Her inspirational and empowering approach has been helping people all over the world for over 20 years. Her books, articles, poetry, and songs have been published locally and internationally. Krystal is the co-founder of New Day Counseling in Michigan. For information on her best-selling books, visit http://www.amazon.com/Krystal-Kuehn/e/B0074OI67O.
Her web sites include: Christian-Kindle-Books.com, BeHappy4Life.com, NewDayCounseling.org,

NewSongProductions.com, Baby-Poems.com as well as Facebook.com/WordsOfInspiration, and Be Your Best Blog.

#4: Honoring A Christmas Kindness

By Carol Freed

My first Christmas away from home...what could have been lonely became an opportunity to learn a lesson that has influenced my behavior for the past 50 years.

My holiday plans began to take shape with no hint of what was to come. I had been working as a secretary for the government in Washington DC since my high school graduation in Florida the prior June. My youthful energy and enthusiasm led me to volunteer to be the secretary-on-duty on Christmas Day.

With my meager salary, buying a car was not yet possible. I rode city busses everywhere; however, the church I attended was not on a bus line, so a retired couple drove me to church. Naturally, I told them about not going home at Christmas. To my surprise, they graciously invited me to stay overnight with them on Christmas Eve and go to work on Christmas Day after having breakfast with them. This sounded wonderful, so I accepted the invitation.

After I got home from work on the 24th I walked over to their house. To my delight, I stepped into an atmosphere unlike anything I had ever experienced! Their older, brick, two-story home, decorated so beautifully, could have been featured in a magazine.

Every piece of holiday décor reflected a lifetime of memories shared by this couple and their now-grown children. Their live

Christmas tree almost touched the high ceiling, proudly displaying hand-made ornaments. I had never lived in a home with a fireplace, so I kept staring at the crackling fire beneath a mantle with family pictures and candles.

The warmth and friendliness of my hosts completed this magical atmosphere. Dinner featured farm-country foods I remembered from my childhood in Minnesota - ham, sweet potatoes, homemade bread and jam and juicy sweet apple pie. The years have dimmed my memory of how we spent Christmas Eve, but I clearly remember sleeping on their sofa, where I could inhale the aromas of their hospitality.

Much to my surprise, the next morning when I looked outside, big lazy flakes of snow were weaving a new white blanket that covered the city. I had not seen snow for the seven years I lived in Florida. Staring out their large front window at the peaceful scene made me look like a grown-up kid ~ with my eyes wide open and a big smile.

Before leaving Christmas morning, I thanked my hostess for allowing me to share such a beautiful time with them. I expressed regret that I could not think of an adequate way to show my appreciation. She replied, "Every time you help someone through your life, consider it as a thank you to us. That will be the best way for you to remember us."

Countless times in the years since then I have dedicated a kindness to my Christmas hosts. Eventually their hospitality formed the basis for launching a ministry called Heritage House in Bend, Oregon. This renovated older home provided a warm and peaceful atmosphere to families who were in town due to a medical emergency of a loved one – a shelter in their storm. The Heritage House served hundreds of guests - far beyond what my Christmas hostess could ever have imagined.

Since then, the concept of "paying it forward" is well known, but for me at age 18, the suggestion of my hostess became a foundational model in my life.

In 2012, I self-published my first Kindle ebook through Amazon. The title reflects the many ways I give Encourage-Mints (give a mint, refresh a life). These mints are not just random acts of kindness but result from listening to the promptings of the Holy Spirit about who to help and what they need. I start each day asking the same question Saul asked Jesus on the road to Damascus, "Lord, what do you want me to do?" Acts 9:6 NKJ

Sometimes I give a mint to a stressed clerk in a store, or perhaps a hug or listening ear to a friend going through a tough time, or crying with a grieving mom by our shopping carts. My favorite encourage-mints involve giving a cuddly Teddy bear ~ a prayer bear ~ to someone who is sick or going through a tough time ~ to remind them of all the people who are praying for them.

These meetings are not by chance but are my close encounters of the God kind. I continue to listen to the Holy Spirit as he guides me to the people I can help. Isaiah 30:21 says it well: "Whether you turn to the right or to the left, your ears will hear a voice inside you saying, 'This is the way. Walk in it'."

Telling this story gives me another way to thank my hostess. She answered my prayer to not be alone that Christmas and gave me an example of kindness that changed my life.

Bio:
Over 45 years of marriage, raising three sons, volunteering in my community, church and schools has given me endless opportunities to see things as they could be and do the unusual

and unexpected. I have two web sites to encourage Christians worldwide and published an ebook in 2012 "Encourage-Mints."

#5: When We Choose Kindness

By Carol Round

"Command them to do good, to be rich in good deeds, and to be generous and willing to share"— 1 Timothy 6:18 (NIV)

In a hurry at the speedy checkout lane, I was becoming impatient when a problem arose with the person checking out just ahead of me. She had swiped her credit card several times but it wouldn't work. The cashier wasn't having any luck getting it to work either so she called for help.

As I listened to the conversation, I learned the card she was using to pay for her two items was part of a government assistance program. Since it was several days before the end of the month, it dawned on me the customer didn't realize she had used up her monthly allotment. She was going to put the items back when I felt a God nudge.

Reaching into my wallet, I pulled out cash and paid for the two items. The customer protested but I replied, "Please allow me to pay."

Now, here's where the story reveals the story behind the story. The woman was buying ice cream bars. In the past, my attitude would have been, "Well, she's on government assistance. She shouldn't be using the funds to buy ice cream."

Bear with me. Notice, I said in the past. Yes, I was very judgmental before Jesus got hold of me. I still struggle sometimes, but He's not through with me yet. I had first

17

encountered the woman in front of me at the checkout line almost five years earlier. She was seeking help with groceries and some of her past due bills at our church's front door ministry. While our church tries to assist as many as possible, on that particular day, we were out of funds to help with bills. However, we did supply her with food. I recalled her reaction when she learned we were out of funds. It wasn't pleasant. I realized her response on that occasion had affected my attitude toward her.

That day, as I stood in the checkout line, waiting impatiently for my turn, God showed me it didn't matter what this woman was buying. I had an opportunity to be kind. I think I probably received as much pleasure from purchasing her ice cream as she did eating it.

Scottish author and theologian, Ian Maclaren said, "Let us be kind to one another, for most of us are fighting a hard battle." I know I was battling my impatience as I waited my turn to check out that day.

In a sermon titled, "What is Man?" Christian theologian John Wesley said, "You were born for nothing else. You live for nothing else. Your life is continued to you upon earth, for no other purpose than this, that you may know, love and serve God on earth, and enjoy Him to all eternity."

While paying for her ice cream was not a hardship for me, I know God used the incident to help me see another person through His eyes. It was also an opportunity for Him to remind me I'm not here on earth for my own pleasure but to be a servant to others.

Bio:

A retired high school teacher, Carol Round is now pursuing her passion as a syndicated weekly faith-based columnist and is the author of five books. She blogs weekly at www.carolaround.com.

#6: Follow Your Dream

By Joy DeKok

"All our dreams can come true, if we have the courage to pursue them." -Walt Disney

One of my favorite childhood movies was "Follow That Dream" starring Elvis Presley. He sang the theme song liked he meant it. Long after he was gone the words stayed in my heart.

After some harsh comments and negative advice, I had given up writing. I was certain it was over. Forever. The pain of not writing was harder than I thought it would be. My dream was dying a slow death. Every day was one long sigh. I was doing a job I was good at, but didn't like. The lack of hope made it drudgery.

One evening my husband Jon came home from work and after kissing me hello handed me two magazines. For writers. He said, "Joy, please quit your job and follow your dream and write."

Red hot anger raged through me and throwing them at him I said, "I can't." That's not all I said. I ripped myself up one side and down the other. I stomped my foot, and cried. Loud. It was a messy fit with me wiping my nose on my sweatshirt when my hands weren't on my hips. Jon watched me and when he was sure the moment had passed, he silently picked up the magazines and as if the tantrum had never taken place said, "Joy, please quit your job and follow your dream and write."

His quiet, sure belief in me stunned me. It still does.

While we ate supper and as he continued to encourage me, I learned that tuna noodle casserole shared with someone who believes in you is not a mundane meal on a budget, it's five-star delicious. And, that when a man really loves you he will kiss you and tell you he thinks you're beautiful because he can see beyond the red eyes and nose. Plus, drying dishes together is a lovely way to plan ways to make the dream come true.

I had the next day off from work, and was cleaning house when someone rang the doorbell. A delivery man stood on the porch with a new desk and my first word processor. Things were tight for us financially, but Jon still found a way to put his words into action. To honor his generosity, the first document I typed was my resignation. I called Jon to thank him and he said, "I'm praying for you."

Those powerful words felt like warm oil poured over my wounded heart. Comfort and encouragement evicted doubt and despair.

When I said yes to writing, I didn't do it because I believed in me – I did it because Jon believed when I could not. The result surprised us both. His business grew and then expanded. As that happened, he bought me books on the craft of writing, sent me to my first Christian writer's conference, and bought me my first computer – a huge thing that used floppy disks and required I learn a computer language called DOS.

Over the last twenty-five years he has held me when the rejections came, critiques stung, and ideas floundered or failed, and he has kept me supplied in paper and computers (I have a tendency to wear keyboards out). With nine books in print, I still have days when I wonder if I can finish number ten, but the man I married still believes in and prays for me.

When the fear nags at me, Jon smiles and says, "Think on these things. . ." With these gentle words, an unearthly peace floods my soul and I return to my work infused by the words of God in Philippians 4: 6-8 (NLT)...

"Don't worry about anything; instead, pray about everything. Tell God what you need, and thank him for all he has done. Then you will experience God's peace, which exceeds anything we can understand. His peace will guard your hearts and minds as you live in Christ Jesus. And now, dear brothers and sisters, one final thing. Fix your thoughts on what is true, and honorable, and right, and pure, and lovely, and admirable. Think about things that are excellent and worthy of praise."

Jon's Christ-like attitude and steadfast example has birthed tenderness in me toward others who are giving up and whose dreams are gasping for air. His courage in the face of my tantrum and tenderness in my times of stress enables me to say to others, "Please – find a way to follow your dream." When it's my privilege to encourage someone in their journey by sharing Jon's words with them, in my heart I can hear Elvis sing, ". . .you gotta follow that dream wherever that dream may lead. . ."

Watching Jon live his dreams and help others live theirs, I've come to believe that dream followers can change the world for good by gently offering hope to one broken dreamer at a time.

Bio:
Joy DeKok lives with her husband and their two dogs in SE MN. When she's not writing, she's wandering their land on her

John Deere Gator, taking pictures, and praying. You can learn more about her at www.joydekok.com or www.booksbyjoy.com.

#7: Our Gift from God

By Victoria Pitts Caine

Isaiah 43:5 Fear not: for I am with thee: I will bring thy seed from the east, and gather thee from the west. (KJV)

In 1955, when I was six years old, a miraculous event took place half a world away. Bertha and Harry Holt brought eight children into their Oregon home from Korea. While adoption from another country is common place now, that wasn't the case nearly sixty years ago.

Mrs. Holt sought out instruction from God to bring her adopted children to the United States and taking her Bible into her hands, her eyes fell upon Isaiah 43:5.

The Holts paved the way for many couples to adopt and Holt International Children's Services was born. When Harry died in 1964, and many thought the agency they had started would close, Mrs. Holt said, "This work was always God's work. If He wants it to continue, it will."

In 1976, we found out just how important God's work would be to our family. Due to complications from my ruptured appendix, biological children weren't an option. We looked into local adoption and were put on lists, we had sent for information from an adoption agency that served our area, but for a young couple the cost was prohibitive. We had almost given up when the Lord stepped in and we were connected through a Christian friend to the Holt agency. God is good and he led us to the Holts. Because of their kindness and generosity and their unfailing attempts to bring children home to their forever families, including getting congress to pass much needed laws, my husband and I adopted two girls from Korea in 1978 and 1980.

We had already started our giving back journey, as founders of a local adoptive parent organization and volunteering with a national adoption agency to do their international adoption orientation meetings when we were notified by the main office of the Holt agency that Bertha Holt would be in our area and would like to stay in our home. She was every bit the gracious Godly woman we'd expected to meet.

Mrs. Holt gave us the courage to fight for couples waiting for the arrival of children from other countries including a deposition given to the Immigration and Naturalization Service requesting the process of fingerprinting to be expedited.

We believe in sharing God's gifts and during the years after completing our adoptions, we continued to give back to waiting children through Holt sponsorships. We've sponsored babies from Korea and Thailand until their circumstances changed either by adoption or returning home to their biological parents. In the last few years we've sponsored children in China. Last year it was one sibling in a set of twins who were born in prison. When they were moved into another situation, we started sponsoring a pre-teen girl.

Many people tell us that they are in awe of us for what we've done and continue to do through adoption and sponsorships. This always surprises us. We're the lucky ones. Giving back to God's children is a demonstration of our faith and love for the Lord. We don't look upon it as our gift but as a gift we receive. The rewards are tenfold.

Bio:

Victoria Pitts Caine is a native Californian and lives in the bountiful San Joaquin Valley. Her varied interests include genealogy and exotic gemstone collecting both of which she's incorporated into her novels. While her genre is inspirational, she likes to refer to herself as a Christian Romance Adventure Novelist.

#8: The Mortgage Check

By Ruth O'Neil

"God works in mysterious ways" is a statement we have probably all heard. I will be the first to admit that is definitely an understatement! I have had the privilege of receiving God's blessings in ways I never thought possible. I would hear stories of God working, but I had never experienced that for myself, until...

My husband had been out of work because of a herniated disk in his back. He missed six weeks of work at first. That alone was bad enough, but this was over Christmas and we hadn't bought all of our presents yet and our plans to go out of town to see my family had to be canceled. My husband went back to work for one week and was out for three more. His doctor scolded him for going back to work and basically fired him from his job. If he didn't quit and give his back a chance to heal he'd have to have surgery.

It didn't take long for him to find a job he could do. The only problem with it was that there was far less money coming into our checking account than there was going out each month. Things got very hard for us, but we made it a point to remain faithful to God.

We were never ones to broadcast the difficulties going on in our house. Where we grew up, affairs of the home were kept at home. When we moved to another state, we found ourselves living near people whose household affairs were practically announced on highway billboards! It seemed to us that people

27

would cry about their difficulties, while holding their hands out waiting for donations to start pouring in, and often times they did!

My husband and I were opposite of that. We kept everything to ourselves, not even our own family members knew the extent of the financial straits we were in. One night, I spoke to my husband about our mortgage payment. It was going to be the first time in thirteen years we were ever thirty days late, but there was nothing we could do except pray. And pray we did!

Throughout the night, when I wasn't sleeping, I recalled a conversation a truly godly woman had with me one time. She had made the statement, "Pray so big so that when it does happen you know it was God." That got me to thinking. I didn't know anyone who was wealthy enough to pay our mortgage on top of their own bills. I didn't know anyone from who I could borrow money to pay it; that would also require telling someone. I did have a couple of friends that I would ask to pray on occasion.

The next morning, I emailed those two closes friends to pray also. I did not give them any details about the situation, I just said, "Pray!" Within two hours, our church secretary called and said, "I have someone here that wants to make your house payment. They just need to know how much it is." I couldn't answer her for all my blubbering! She apologized saying, "I am so sorry to upset you. I had no idea things were that bad." I was finally able to tell her, "I'm crying because it was God. No one knows how bad our situation is."

God answered our prayer. He knew we were in need when no one else did. We just needed to have the faith that God would provide for us and keep our focus on Him, no matter how difficult things may have been. We couldn't allow ourselves to be pulled away from Him. We knew that not focusing on God would eventually pull us apart as a family, and that was something we would not accept.

To this day we have no idea who helped us and we probably never will. It isn't important. I do know they must be very close to God. They listened carefully to His voice and the specific instructions He gave. The only person we spoke to about our needs was God. He heard and answered our prayers.

This whole experience made me want to secretly reach out to others when I hear of something they need or a difficult time they are going through. Unless you have been the recipient of such generosity, you have no idea what a blessing it is. On the other hand, if you have been the giver, you know what a blessing that can be also. For as great as our blessing was "it is more blessed to give than receive" (Acts 20:35).

Bio:
Ruth O'Neil has been writing for 20-plus years, publishing hundreds of articles in dozens of publications. Her first novel Come Eat at My Table came out earlier this year. When she's not writing, Ruth spends her time quilting, reading, scrapbooking, camping and hiking with her family.

#9: The Overflowing Cup

By Lisa Belcastro

I had come into some money. Not enough to buy a house or fancy car, but a little over fifteen thousand dollars. I sat down at my kitchen table to write out my deposit slip, and my tithing check, and a voice inside my head kept repeating, "Your cup runneth over, your cup runneth over."

I know that verse well. I have a framed picture hanging in my home with the twenty-third Psalm written on the image. I have prayed Psalm 23 in times of sorrow and times of joy. I have offered up the words in thankfulness, and prayed them in an hour of need when I felt as though I was walking through the valley of the shadow of death.

That afternoon, in the quiet of my home, I offered up the following line, "Surely goodness and mercy shall follow me all the days of my life and I shall dwell in the house of the Lord forever. Thank you, Lord, for filling my cup to overflowing."

When I finished praying, images of a teacher at my daughter's school flashed before eyes. I knew her. "Ann" taught one of my daughter's extracurricular classes. I couldn't shake the feeling that God was calling me to give Ann some money. I didn't want to offend her, I didn't know if she needed money, and I didn't know why me as opposed to one of her friends. But, I couldn't shake the feeling that I was being called to help her.

After prayerful consideration, I wrote Ann a check, enclosed with a card that read: "My cup runneth over. I believe God wants me to share His blessings with you."

I dropped the card off at school that afternoon when I picked up my daughter. Later that night, I received a teary phone call. Ann asked how I knew she was desperate. I told her I didn't know. She then shared with me a series of problems that had besieged her over the last few months. She was broke. She couldn't pay her rent and had received two warning notices. Ann told me the check I'd sent her would pay her rent and buy much-needed groceries for her family. And, she knew another woman whose husband had just left her and she was going to take ten percent of the money I'd given her and bless someone else.

I hung up the phone, visibly shaken. I'd had no idea. And then it hit me, I felt blessed, blessed beyond words to have been able to help another mom. And I would have never known about Ann's need if God had not impressed upon me the image of sending her a check.

I thanked God for His clear direction and offered up a song of praise for His goodness and mercy. My eyes were filled with tears, grateful that He allowed me to bless another with what He had blessed me.

Every day I walk by the scenic image with the words that remind me that God will always meet my needs.

"The Lord is my shepherd, I shall not want. He maketh me to lie down in green pastures: he leadeth me beside the still waters. He restoreth my soul: he leadeth me in the paths of righteousness for his name's sake. Yea, though I walk through the valley of the shadow of death, I will fear no evil: for thou art with me; thy rod and thy staff they comfort me. Thou preparest a table before me in the presence of mine enemies: thou anointest my head with oil; my cup runneth over. Surely goodness and mercy shall follow me all the days of my life: and I will dwell in the house of the Lord forever."

Bio:

Lisa Belcastro is an author, Christ-follower, mommy and wife, marathon runner, chocolate lover, beach goer, avid gardener and person to one orange kitty named Ben. Lisa's current releases are Shenandoah Nights, Shenandoah Crossings and the upcoming Shenandoah Dreams.

#10: A Bruised Reed

By Graham Roberts

'Jesus said' and again 'Jesus said'.

The words resonated in my mind. I had heard them – maybe not in the ordinary audible way but I had heard them.

In that micro-second my entire life and world changed. From a person of no faith, no beliefs and a mocking disregard for Christianity, I suddenly knew beyond any reason that Jesus was alive, was real and had somehow reached out to me!

In a very short time the 'old me' had gone and I became a totally new person. I became a person with a new found set of values, a new understanding of the world and a keen knowledge of sin.
It's not that I didn't continue to sin – it's more that I knew when I did and felt it very keenly.

Within a few months I felt almost like a stranger looking in at my 'new' life. I had got up and left my job and started my own company with a friend.

One of the most important things I did at this time was to start a charity (non-profit organization) to help those in need.

The company grew rapidly and was soon turning over about £1.5m ($3m) a year. I was able to help lots of people, buy family cars, buy strangers computers and other things and I was able to put money anonymously through people's doors.

Things were good but something deep inside told me there was a flaw somewhere. I couldn't work it out but, despite the outward success, something was amiss.

Eventually I found that my 'friend' and business partner had been working behind my back to take over the business all for himself. He manipulated me into a position where I couldn't carry on doing my work. I didn't mind so much about the loss of my company, the loss of my income and the loss of any 'status'. I was hurt by the betrayal of my 'friend'.

I lost virtually everything and my anxiety and sense of betrayal led me into a deep depression.

As I spent lonely nights fighting the demons of despair I reached for my Bible and read Matthew 12. Verse 20. 'A bruised reed He will not break'. I had been very, very close to the end but this verse gave me a rock to stand on and my faith deepened as I gradually clawed my way out of the depression and managed to get some semblance of life back.

I started to work full time for the charity. Working in a charity shop was not something I had ever envisaged or wanted to do. I didn't know how to stand behind a counter and serve people. I was used to being served!

But, and this is a huge 'but' – I loved the work, I loved the interaction and I felt it was an enormous honor and blessing to be placed in a situation where I could really help others in a tangible way. This might not mean buying them things – it could be listening to their problems and having a real empathy with them.

The charity has grown quickly since I became involved. We now have two shops, run a food bank, community events and are recognized and respected by the local authorities and the general public.

Personally I have written five books on topics such as Christianity, poetry and a children's story.

I will never be pleased that I was betrayed in such a way by somebody I trusted but I now see that the love outplayed has now left me in a higher place.

What did Jesus say? Well I have the feeling it was 'follow me'!

Bio:
I am the founder and administrator of The BASIC Life Charity (www.basic.org.uk). Business And Service In Christ. I have written Christian songs and books. My song 'I Just Want to Stay' has been adopted by the death row support charity Human Writes (www.humanwrites.org). I come from Felixstowe, Suffolk, UK.

#11: The Christmas We Won't Forget

By Marilynn Dawson

It was either 2004 or 2005, and it would be the Christmas we'd talk about around the table for years to come. As was the case every year, Christmastime was lean. Once again, I had hardly bought the kids anything. Then an envelope showed up in the mail as the Christmas shopping season began. It was for the local gospel mission and they wanted funds to pay for Christmas dinner that year. My son insisted that we send enough for three plates. A check was written and I delivered it to their office.

A week or so later it was my daughter's birthday in mid-November. She received birthday money and suddenly got the idea to go shopping for a non-perishable Christmas dinner hamper for the food bank. We bought enough to put three Christmas dinner food hampers together and delivered it to the local food bank.

What should be waiting for us on the steps to our front door when we returned that day, but the biggest food hamper I'd seen yet!!! Included in that hamper were grocery cards, tripling what had been given to the gospel mission earlier that month! But it wasn't over. . .

Word arrived that my brother wouldn't be able to come for Christmas due to lack of funds for gas. Work in December had picked up a bit and I sent him money to gas up his truck and head out for Christmas.

Christmas Day arrived and everyone gathered at my parents' place, including family friends. Dinner was enjoyed and then we all sat around my parents' Christmas forest (they didn't just have one tree. . .) to read the Christmas story out of Luke 2, and to open gifts. The family friends handed me an envelope containing such a large gas card, that it would take the next four months to spend it all!

A fourth event had occurred as well, for which God had multiplied the blessing that year, causing me to express a mild case of frustration that I couldn't give without it coming back to me. My son couldn't help commenting in his elementary-school-aged way, that I seemed "happy-angry". It proved to be a teaching moment that none of us will ever forget, as I explained to my kids that you can never out-give God! God says in Luke 6:38, "Give, and it shall be given unto you; good measure, pressed down, and shaken together, and running over, shall men give into your bosom. For with the same measure that ye mete withal it shall be measured to you again."

God challenges His people in Malachi 3:10, "Bring ye all the tithes into the storehouse, that there may be meat in mine house, and prove me now herewith, saith the LORD of hosts, if I will not open you the windows of heaven, and pour you out a blessing, that there shall not be room enough to receive it."

The blessings showered on our family have generally not been of the financial variety, but God has always made sure our needs were met, even to the point of throwing in extras here and there.

I don't know what God will do this Christmas, but I do know He loves gift-giving even more than we do! So when you're out there deciding what to get for who, don't forget the homeless, don't forget the hard-up, buy for them just as you'd buy for rich Uncle Joe, and see what God does in return! Don't give to get mind you, that's not what I'm advocating. Just keep your eyes open. Perhaps for you too, this will be a Christmas you'll never forget for years to come.

Bio:
Marilynn Dawson is the author of "Becoming the Bride of Christ: A Personal Journey" and "Mom's Little Black Book: Godly Advice for the High School Graduate".

#12: Absolutely Blown Away!

By Brenda McGraw

God is faithful! I know we all have different stories in our life where we have seen the faithfulness of God. This story is no different, it just happens to be one of mine. My name is Brenda and back in 2003 I went through a divorce after 23 years of marriage. Suddenly, I found myself all alone with two children. My daughter had been attending a Christian school at our Church since she was in the 6th grade. At this current time, she was a rising 10th grader. Since my husband left in 2002, I had been under a real financial hardship. It was our desire to keep my daughter at her school, but financially the budget wasn't sufficient to pay the tuition.

As registration was quickly approaching for the upcoming school year, I was praying about what to do and how I was going to get the money to cover her tuition. Her dad had left us financially drained due to his addiction to prescription drugs and before he left, our home life had become devastating.

I had an opportunity that summer to go on a Mission Trip to New Hampshire with my Church. Generous members who wanted to support me, paid for my trip in full. Whenever I go on a Mission Trip, I always know God has a purpose for me attending and serving. I will pray and ask God what my purpose is on this trip and how He plans to use me.

One day during the trip, it was pouring down rain and our service project for that day was cancelled because of the rain. Therefore, our leader decided we would take this opportunity to spend time in prayer. He asked if anyone could share any prayer requests. After hearing others sharing, I mentioned that I was praying about my daughter's school tuition situation. Everyone prayed. The next day I was pulled aside by one of the men on the trip, whom I had never met before the trip. He told me that he had worked it out with his company to pay my daughter's tuition in full for the next year. This was over $3500! I was absolutely blown away with shock and excitement!

We are all provided opportunities to be a blessing to other people. Possibly, we all can't provide a financial blessing like we were blessed with that year, but God gives to each of us individually, so we can bless others. We will never be aware of the needs of others, unless we listen intently to what people say. People will share their needs with us in conversation, but most of the time we are not listening very well. Pray and ask God to give you an opportunity to be a blessing to someone. Then open your ears and your heart to those who you meet during that day. Next comes the best part...take action. Do something! Be a blessing!

"And God will generously provide all you need. Then you will always have everything you need and plenty left over to share with others." (2 Corinthians 9:8 NLT)

Unfortunately, because we are all so busy taking care of our own business; we often don't see the needs of others. I truly believe that God blessed us with the generosity of this man during our difficult time, because God blesses faithfulness. I strive to be faithful to God. I chose to go on this trip and serve others. Like I mentioned, I prayed and asked God what my purpose was on this trip. We had a wonderful trip and made some great contacts for the Church we were serving. However, I truly believe on this particular trip, the purpose for me going was not only for me to serve, but for God to once again show His faithfulness and provision to me and my family.

God answered my prayer and I thanked Him! I share this testimony now, still thanking Him, and giving Him praise. When we share our testimonies with others, it is one way we can give God all the glory! It is through the hope we find in Christ that we are able to share hope with others! I encourage you to thank God today for answered prayers and ask Him to show you opportunities so you can be a blessing to others.

Bio:
Brenda McGraw shares hope and truth through life lessons on her website, "Ask God Today". She is a wife, mom of 5, a Nonnie, and a Cancer and Heart Attack survivor. Brenda is in the process of writing her first book, "Joy Beyond."

You can contact her through:
www.askgodtoday.com
Twitter - @BrendaMMcGraw
Facebook Page:
https://www.facebook.com/askgodtodaybyBrenda

#13: The Generosity of Adoption

By Beth Willis Miller

In many ways, it's still a mystery...how I came to be. I met my birthmother, Lydia, in 1983, when I was 30 years old, and Lydia was 72. Lydia explained to me the circumstances of my conception, birth, and adoption. During a Memorial Day holiday get-away weekend with a gentleman in 1952, Lydia, at age 41, became pregnant with me. When she realized she was pregnant, she told the gentleman with whom she had spent the weekend and he was unwilling to help her. Her mother, Vincenza, did not want her daughter, a single mother at age 41, to disgrace her family with an illegitimate child, so Lydia left Chicago to live with a relative in Miami, Florida.

In October, around the time of Columbus Day, she went to a back-alley abortionist to abort me, but when the abortionist examined her and realized she was over four months pregnant, he told her the abortion might kill her, and he refused to do it. Lydia made arrangements with the Salvation Army hospital in Jacksonville to give me up for adoption. On Friday the 13th she gave birth to me, and signed the papers giving me up for adoption on Valentine's Day 1953.

Through the generosity of my loving Christian adoptive parents, my life was changed forever when they adopted me on Easter weekend 1953. I grew up in church, active in Sunday School and missions organizations. I prayed to receive Jesus Christ as my Lord and Savior at the age of 10. I married Jack Miller on Mother's Day 1973 and finished my bachelor's degree in education in 1975, and my master's degree in education in 1977. Our daughter, Tracy, was born in 1979, and our son, Jason, was born in 1991, and in 2012 our daughter Tracy and her husband, Zac, blessed us with an adorable grandson, Colton.

After serving in various teaching and supervisory positions, I was selected as the state consultant for gifted education programs by the Florida Department of Education in Tallahassee, and other leadership roles. I grow closer to my Lord and Savior Jesus Christ every day through prayer, worship, and the study of His Word. I rest and find comfort in these life verses: "For I know the plans I have for you," says the Lord. "They are plans for good and not for disaster, to give you a future and a hope." (Jeremiah 29:11) "You made all the delicate, inner parts of my body and knit me together in my mother's womb. Thank you for making me so wonderfully complex! Your workmanship is marvelous—how well I know it. You watched me as I was being formed in utter seclusion, as I was woven together in the dark of the womb. You saw me before I was born. Every day of my life was recorded in your book. Every moment was laid out before a single day had passed." (Psalm 139:13-16)

I believe in the sovereignty of God, that nothing comes into my life that is not filtered through God's hands of love. I believe there are no "accidents." I believe God planned who my birth parents would be and who my generous adoptive Mom and Dad would be, and both influences, plus His, are needed to help me become all that He created me to be. I believe that God sees the end from the beginning. He knows me intimately, He knit me together in my mother's womb, one day I will see Him face-to-face and I will know as I am known...until then, I will expect a mystery. It is His plan that's important, not my desire.

I didn't bring myself into this world, and I can't take myself into heaven. I really don't know what is best for me or for those I love. I ask God to make me sensitive to the reality that He is in control, and that He is using this--even this--to conform me to the image of His Son. I want that most of all. I train my mind to acknowledge God's hand in whatever it is I'm living with. I practice words like, "I don't know," "I will trust," "I can't explain," "I release it all," because God is sovereign. He is the beginning, He will be the ending, and in between, by His grace, He lets us be part of His perfect plan, for His glory and for our good. In the meantime, I will expect a mystery.

Bio:
Beth Willis Miller, M.Ed., co-author of Under His Wings—Healing Truth for Adoptees of All Ages and member of AWSA, the Advanced Writers and Speakers Association. Beth has a Master's degree in Education, in curriculum, instruction, and supervision. She is married with two adult children, and one grandson.

Blog: http://bethwillismiller.blogspot.com
About me: http://about.me/bethwillismiller
Facebook: https://www.facebook.com/bethwillismillerauthor
Amazon: http://www.amazon.com/Beth-Willis-Miller/e/B008OMTMXC

#14: He Wanted to Know the Man Upstairs

By Gerald Bergeron

I was a shipping clerk, my job was to load and unload trucks. The thing I loved the most about this job was I could give the good news of Christ to every trucker who came to be loaded.

A few truckers were also employed at this company. Yet even though we talked sometimes, it all added to small talk. One person, and I will not give his real name, had listened to me preach many times. He never seemed to be interested though, so I never really pushed the Gospel on him.

One day to my surprise, he caught me off guard, as he approached the Hilo I was driving, "Jerry can you tell me what you know about the man upstairs." Well I thought to myself, he must want to know if God is real or not, yet something in my spirit told me something else was bothering him. I began to explain what I could, with the time I had, and he seemed to be OK with the words I was telling him.

A few weeks later, there was a layoff, and his job was on the line. Ultimately, he was laid off and I wondered why he was so concerned about God and wanting to know if he really was up there as he referred to the "man upstairs."

Another trucker told me this person was in the hospital getting a test done. I asked what was wrong yet no one knew what the test was for, so I just prayed for him and went about my work. About a week later another friend told me that the person I prayed for was now in the hospital, he was dying of leukemia. My heart sunk to my feet; why did I not pray with him for his salvation?

Then I heard God speak to my heart, "he needs to hear the message of salvation." Was there time I wondered, and what would I say? I thought about the verse in Romans 10: 9-10, "If you will confess with your mouth and believe in your heart…" This was a wonderful message in its entirety yet he had never heard about salvation nor God for that matter, except the little bit I told him about.

Then I felt God move in my spirit, and the small voice inside me said, "Go." Though fear said he would not receive, faith would have me believe he would. I found out which hospital he was at and went to bring the good news to someone who needed to receive a blessing that only God could give.

When I arrived to his room, another coworker was there. I pushed aside all fear and began to tell this person about the grace of God and the life he would enter if he would receive Jesus into his life.
He told me "I never even knew there would be a life after this one." So after telling him about Jesus, I invited him to receive Jesus into his life, and moments later, he gave his life to Jesus.

A few days later I called his wife, after getting the number from a friend, to see how he was doing. She informed me that he died, and though I was crying in my heart for this new brother in Christ, I knew he was now walking those streets of gold. I learned a very important lesson, as God showed me, that we must always be willing to offer His grace as he touches lives.

"But I would not have you to be ignorant, brethren, concerning them which are asleep, that ye sorrow not, even as others which have no hope." 1Thessalonians 4:13

I must say I still cry in my heart for this person, but I have learned that as the angels in heaven rejoice over one sinner who repents, I too can rejoice. AMEN

Bio:
I am the author of seven Christian books and a bible study journal. I have written poetry and have two poetry books. I am married with three sons and a daughter.

#15: Generosity Toward God

By Brad Francis

"I will not offer burnt offerings to the Lord my God that cost me nothing." (2 Sam. 24:24 ESV)

How many times has that verse gone through my head? The words were originally spoken by King David. His sinful pride had brought judgment onto the nation of Israel, but God relented in the punishment to spare His people as David repented. Obediently seeking restoration, the king went to the owner of a threshing floor and offered to buy the land to build an offering to sacrifice to the Lord.

When the owner of the threshing floor, a man named Araunah, learned why David wanted the area, he offered everything for free: the land, the material for the altar, the oxen for the sacrifice. I've always admired Araunah for that. Surely, the king could afford to pay him a generous price, but Araunah did not seek to profit off the exchange.

David, however, knew the meaning of the word sacrifice. He had sinned and it was his place to build the altar and honor God with the burnt offering. He insisted on paying Araunah because he wanted to offer God his best—not simply re-gifting the Almighty with someone else's generosity.

Like David, I don't want to give to God what cost me nothing.

But what do you give the Creator who owns "the cattle on a thousand hills"? (Psalm 50:10 ESV)

Well, you give to the people He created, of course. And the wonderful truth is that each gift is an opportunity to share the love of Christ and maybe even the Gospel with someone who needs it.

My family and I were traveling from our current home in Indiana up to Michigan to see our families. This trip was unique because we started it right: by praying, in the van while traveling, that God would give us opportunities to serve Him and share His love with someone while on this trip.

Even as I type it here, I'm a bit disinclined to believe my own memory. The trip took about four hours without stops. We've had much longer car trips, but I'm not the sort of person who wants to take the scenic route when I've got four hours to go. So even sincerely praying that prayer was a bit of a victory for me.

And, in my experience, this is one prayer that the Lord is almost always willing to answer.

On this trip, it was a broken down car on the side of the road.

Let me point out right here that I am the grandson of a master mechanic, a man who had loads of experience working for major auto makers and in smaller garages. If a quarter of that hands-on knowledge trickled down to my dad, I don't think any of it found its way to me.

It makes a wonderful excuse when I see a car pulled over with its hazards on, to tell you the truth. What in the world would I have to offer them? I can barely change a headlight, I'll tell myself.

But you can't just pass by someone in need after specifically asking God to give you opportunities. You can't do it. And, in this instance, we pulled over and I jumped out to greet two guys who were horribly embarrassed because their issue wasn't all that complicated after all: they had run out of gas, and they didn't have the money to put any more in.

Despite my oh-so-earnest prayer, however, this sort of thing is hard for me. I usually don't worry about finances at all. My wife does enough of that for both of us. And yet she's much more willing to give in this sort of situation than I am. I can't even put a finger on why I have a hard time with it. I know there are some out there who are yelling at the page (or e-reader), telling me that these people are charlatans looking to bamboozle me into a hand-out without being in need at all, but that's not where my hold-up is.

You see, I'm only doing it partially for them. I'm doing it for God. And am I going to offer something to the Lord that costs me nothing?

And the part I'm doing for them? It's to show them the love of Jesus Christ and, if the Holy Spirit provides the opportunity, to share the Gospel with them. Scam artists need that just as much as people in need, as far as I can tell.

So we got a gas can and put enough in their car to get them to the gas station off the highway. When we got there, I filled their tank up, even though they didn't need that much to get to their destination. I was able to buy them dinner, even if it was only gas station food. And I did it all because, when they thanked me profusely, I was able to say, "Don't worry about it. I was praying that God would give us an opportunity to share His love with someone. We're Christians, and this is the best way I know to share the love of Jesus. So don't feel bad—you're an answer to prayer."

I'd like to report that they bowed their knees and turned to Jesus Christ as Savior and Lord there in the Speedway parking lot. They didn't, but I'd like to report it. I have no idea how the Holy Spirit may have used the encounter, however, and how He may still be using it today.

Salvation, after all, is His business. My job is to be obedient, and I think I was.

I think this encounter sticks in my mind because, at that point, it was the most I had ever spent helping out a stranger in need simply to do so in the name of Christ. But Jesus instructed us to "make friends for yourselves by means of unrighteous wealth" with an eye on eternity (Luke 16:9 ESV) and I think this is what He meant.

I don't have a great deal of wealth by this country's standard, and yet I have never missed a meal because I was generous to someone in the name of Jesus Christ.

And even if I did have to sacrifice to give a gift to my Lord? That seems wholly appropriate. After all, I will not offer Him something that cost me nothing.

Bio:
Brad Francis likes to write to glorify God. He is the author of the best-selling short story The Book of the Harvest, the Christian fantasy series The Magi Chronicles, and the satirical novel The Savvy Demon's Guide to Godly Living. You can learn more about him and his books at Christfictionandvideogames.blogspot.com.

#16: Pecans In Heaven

By Charles W. Page

Have you ever wondered if there will be pecans in heaven? I have. In fact, my obsession with pecans has been driving me nuts. In addition to having a heavenly taste, pecans are loaded with unsaturated fats and antioxidants. Pecans are good for your heart! Being a health conscious doctor, I try to eat an extra serving of Buttered Pecan ice cream every chance I get. I want to give my old ticker every opportunity to be healthy. Having an extra spare tire to carry around makes your heart work harder. It's almost like I am exercising around the clock. More exercise is a good thing—right? So, here's to another scoop of pecans loaded with cream and sugar!

A "grave" thought:

Over the years, I have come to terms with a painful truth; every patient I treat will someday stop breathing, turn cold and die. The scriptures remind us that if we are born once, then we will die twice; but if we are born twice then we will only experience death once. There are things that matter more than when or how we die: where we are headed and what we leave behind. Hopefully, what is left behind is a legacy of faithfulness. In the case of Katherine, she left behind little sacks of pecans.

Two dreaded words:

That night I had to tell them the brutal, honest truth: "its cancer". Katherine came to the emergency room with a locally advanced breast cancer, invading the muscles of her chest, eroding through her skin, weeping through her clothes.

After years of hiding her illness from her family, her secret was exposed and she was whisked to the ER. Katherine and I knew the truth; there was no emergency. The tumor had been there for years. Her disease was far too extensive for a surgical cure. The family was devastated at the news; Katherine was not surprised at all. Strangely, she accepted the news with an odd, heartwarming smile. Everyone was asking the same question. Why would someone wait until it was too late?

When all else fails: bribe your doctor:

Journeying the dark road of cancer with her, I began to understand that Katherine was far from living in denial. Believing that her life was a gift from God, she knew that her task was almost completed. With each visit, she would bring her gift with her to the office. Disarming her physician with pecans, she could then steer the conversation towards her passion—picking pecans. When the cancer grew in the lymph nodes under her arm, her "picking arm" began to swell. Her concern was not about her prognosis or the side effects of radiation. Instead, we discussed whether it was safe for her to continue picking pecans in the Angelina river bottom.

Katherine lived to pick pecans. Walking down by the river, Katherine picked up pecans, having sweet times of fellowship with Jesus. As she worked and worshipped, people and situations came to mind. Praying by the muddy waters of the river, picking pecans, she would receive counsel, encouragement and direction from above. Her life flowed from her abiding communion with the rivers of living water that flowed from within. Disrupting that connection was worse than death itself. So, we let her continue picking pecans.

The tables turn:

During this time my mother, who never smoked, developed a chronic cough. Failing to follow up with her doctor, she was diagnosed with an advanced, rare type of lung cancer. Grieving with regret, I watched my mother shrivel away after each dose of chemotherapy. My faith began to be shaken. I had seen the last stages of cancer too many times. Surgery enabled me to "heal with steal": performing life-saving surgeries on cancer patients. Yet I was totally incapable of doing anything for my own mother. I was becoming a wounded healer.

I began to notice with each visit that there was a striking resemblance between Katherine and my mother: their perspectives on living and giving, their unselfish concern towards others, their presentation with cancer too far advanced to cure, their ability to find joy amidst pain and suffering.

Psychologists call it transference, redirecting your feelings from one person to another. In medical circles transference is considered in a negative light; physicians often lose their objectivity. In a spiritual sense, God was transferring encouragement, hope and healing as I cared for a lady stricken with cancer, giving out little sacks of pecans.

Instead of talking about her prognosis and treatment options on routine visits, Katherine would move the conversation towards my mother: "How is your mother? I pray for her when I'm down by the river."

I visited Katherine one last time in the hospital. She fell and broke her hip while walking in the river bottom. Trying to motivate her to keep going, I asked her to come back to the office and bring some more pecans. We both knew the truth. Her pecan picking days were over. Shortly after our visit, she passed into eternity.

Last fall, her daughter dropped by with a gift: "We promised mother that we would bring you some. One of her last wishes before she passed was that we bring you fresh pecans every year." Those pecans now are frequent reminders, not just of Katherine, but of several truths that we all should consider.

Pecans are reminders that suffering can become wounderful:

Katherine reminds us that our personal suffering can be transformed living in the shadow of the cross. Jesus' horrific death makes sense only when we consider that He suffered so that we could experience forgiveness, wholeness, purpose and contentment. Indeed, He was wounded for our transgressions. Wounderful!

God uses our deepest hurts and disappointments to channel His blessings into the lives of others. As grapes are pulverized into a sweet, refreshing wine, God squeezes rivers of living water out of us through our suffering. The pain we experience is for our good and His glory; it is never wasted when we faithfully abide in the source of life.

Embrace your wounds. Place your pain into the hands of a sovereignly good God. Watch and marvel as the source of life transforms your affliction into a refreshing stream, blessing others around with the refreshing fragrance of grace.

Pecans are good for our hearts:

Who would have ever thought that a sack of pecans would bring spiritual healing? God uses us the most when we recognize it the least, hinting to us that the blessing does not come from ourselves. Katherine's pecans remind us that the obscure, insignificant things in our lives often have the greatest impact in the lives of others. The rivers of living water uncontrollably flow from their source: typically unrecognized by the channel from which it came.

What are your pecans? What are things that God has placed in your hands? Release them into the hands of your Father. Cast them into the uncontrollable current of His sovereign goodness. Watch as others are healed in unimaginable ways by small gifts of sacrificial love.

Our "pecans" can be the tool that God uses to heal hearts: physically, emotionally, psychologically and spiritually. You may find that as you sacrificially give in spite of your suffering, God in turn begins to heal you in ways you never expected.

Pecans remind me of heaven.

If we are painfully honest with ourselves, each one of us lives in some degree of denial: from eating another bowl of ice cream to neglecting the subtle symptoms of cancer. We must not deny the reality that we will all pass into eternity. Unless the Lord delays His return we will all experience the first death.

When I pass into eternity and see the face Jesus, I want Him to take me to the river that flows from the throne of God. On its banks there is a tree, bearing twelve different kinds of fruit, giving healing to the nations. I believe that the tree of life will bear pecans. By the riverside, eating from the tree, the redeemed will finally experience wholeness and healing in its fullness. There I will see Katherine and my mother, holding hands, waiting for me with a handful of pecans.

Bio:
Charles W. Page MD is the author of Surrendered Sleep: A Biblical Perspective. He can be found at www.pagingdrpage.com.

#17: What Goes Around...

By Ann Musico

So often we think the small things we do won't have a powerful effect, but we couldn't be more wrong! God brought the meaning of Job 8:7 to life for me in a beautiful way, which says, "And though your beginning was small, yet your latter end would greatly increase."

A story I read in a ministry magazine about how this woman started a Christian magazine absolutely blessed me. I was inspired by her faith and tenacity and knew immediately that I had to subscribe to her publication. So I did! I awaited the first issue with great excitement. It finally came and I just about devoured it! It was excellent and every article seemed to speak to my spirit. I was so thrilled and looked forward to the next month's issue with anticipation and joy.

Only I waited and waited and it never came. I found an email address in the first issue and emailed asking if there was a problem that was keeping the second issue from coming. Well I received a very gracious email response from the woman who created and published the magazine saying that she had come up against some unforeseen difficulties and sadly would have to suspend publication. She said she would refund every person who'd purchased a subscription and simply apologized and asked for patience as she would be refunding people from her own pocket.

I immediately sent her a response saying that she could consider my subscription fee as a seed sown in her ministry and not to worry about refunding it to me. She replied with gratitude and while I was disappointed because I loved her magazine, I felt that was the end of it. I really didn't feel that $20 seed was much in the overall scheme of things so I really didn't think much more about it.

Well fast forward about 6 months and I got another email from this woman saying the Lord had spoken to her and told her to begin offering daily devotions online and to begin rebuilding her ministry in that way. She asked if I would be interested in subscribing for these free daily devotions. Of course I jumped at the chance and did. I was not disappointed as she shared in such a profound and transparent way whatever the Lord was showing her in her life. It was relevant and I still look forward to receiving them each day, 6 years later.

That seemingly insignificant seed I sowed grew into an amazing tree of blessing through her generosity to me. About two years into receiving her online devotions I started my health coaching business. I noticed that she offered the opportunity to advertise on her daily emails. I contacted her and asked what she would charge for a one month ad. She told me. I was just beginning my business so finances were tight. I was just about ready to email and purchase an ad when she emailed me back and said she'd prayed about it and the Lord told her to put my ad on at no charge! She did just that and most of my earliest clients and newsletter subscribers came directly from her!

She kept the ad for my business on her emails for four years at absolutely no charge! I have, in turn, promoted her products in my book and in my newsletters and I consider her a friend, a great source of encouragement, support and an anointed prayer partner. We have both experienced the reality of Proverbs 11:25: "The generous will prosper; those who refresh others will themselves be refreshed."

A small step of obedience and generosity on my part yielded more than a hundred-fold return!

Bio:
Ann Musico is a holistic health coach who helps women to exemplify lives of vibrant health and wholeness, empowering them to improve their health in a simple and achievable way, enabling them to be catalysts for change in their families, workplaces and communities. Visit her website to learn more: http://www.threedimensionalvitality.com.

#18: Give and It Shall Be Given to You

By Lorine Hyman

"Give, and it will be given to you. A good measure, pressed down, shaken together and running over, will be poured into your lap. For with the measure you use, it will be measured to you." - Luke 6:38

As a clinical psychologist who works in inner city Baltimore, I am frequently told stories about generosity. I have heard stories of rent being paid moments before eviction, organs donated by both loved ones and strangers in order to save a life, and a complete "Christmas" being delivered in the middle of the night to grieving families (decorations, presents and all). So naturally when the call for giving stories arrived, I thought I would share one of these stories. However, after much prayer I decided to share a story of generosity that changed my life.

In addition to being a clinical psychologist specially trained to treat childhood trauma, I am also a foster parent. Like most foster parents, I entered the process thinking I had so much to give to a child in need. Not only had the Lord Jesus blessed me with a wonderful job and home, I had close to 10 years of experience treating children in the foster care system. However, I quickly realized that despite all I had to give to each child placed in my care, they had more to give me. Foster parents are entrusted with raising children at a very vulnerable time in a child's life; each child generously (some more generously than others) entrusts you with their lives. My story of generosity comes from the lives that were entrusted to me. Each child that was placed in my care has helped me grow in my faith in Christ and strengthened my relationship with others (including my own mother). Because of the generosity of the children placed in my life, each of the following lessons were either learned or confirmed:

Each Parent is Doing the Best They Can - When I started out as a foster parent, I did not have the best relationship with my mother. I was raised in a single parent home and did not always understand or agree with the decisions my mother made. If I am honest with myself, I would say I was angry at my mother for some of her decisions. However, my decision to become a foster parent led to me walking in my mother's shoes. While parenting each of my children, I found myself faced with some pretty tough decisions. Looking back, I can say that like my mother I did not always make the best decisions. However, I can honestly say that also like my mother I did the best I could in the moment. So the first generous gift that I was given through the experience of foster care was forgiveness and understanding of my mother. This forgiveness and understanding of my mother has also lead to me assuming that each parent is doing the best they can. I cannot begin to tell you what a difference this has also made in my professional work.

God most often uses humans to answer our prayers – I cannot imagine living through what some of the children who have been placed in my care went through. They have had mothers and fathers who abused them physically and/or sexually. Some of them never knew where their next meal was coming from or watched their parents commit unspeakable crimes. A lot of children in foster care pray that a superhero or prince charming would rescue them. I am neither a superhero nor prince charming, but each child was willing to see me as an answer to their prayers. Do not get me wrong - some of them took longer than others, but in the end they all were willing to trust me and ask for help. This was an important lesson for me to learn because I am pretty independent and would love if Jesus Himself would answer each and every one of my prayers. Despite my desires, God showed me through my children that the same way He used me to answer their prayers, He will use someone to answer my prayers.

God is in Control - The biggest lesson that I learned from my foster children is that God is in control. There are a lot of people making decisions about what is best for each foster child. There is the social worker, social worker supervisor, lawyer, CASA worker, judge, therapist, foster parents, birth parent/family and of course the child. I can honestly say, everyone almost never agreed on what was best. In fact, decisions about placement and what was next were often times of high anxiety. The one thing that gave me and my children comfort was knowing that God was in control. Yes, the judge or caseworker may appear to make the final decision, but I talked to each of my children about how God was not only ultimately making the decision but was working everything out for our good. Even today, in times of high anxiety I draw comfort and peace from the knowledge that God is in control.

To date, I have been given the generous gift of fostering four children. Each year more than 250,000 children in the U.S. enter the foster care system. There are more children entering the system than there are available foster homes. One of my prayers is that more Christians would be willing to step up and help children in crisis by becoming a foster parent. To learn more about becoming a foster parent visit http://www.adoptuskids.org or http://www.nationalococ.org.

Bio:

Corine Hyman is a clinical psychologist who has been helping families for close to 10 years. She enjoys writing picture books that use the Bible to help children and adults understand the biblical basis for why Christians do what they do. You can find her books on Amazon and at www.booksbycorine.com.

#19: A Grateful Mother's Generosity

By Marriott Cole

My grandmother, "Mommer", and Alice's mother, Mrs. Joslyn, were very good friends. They had first met while volunteering for the Red Cross in the Chicago, Illinois area. After Mommer's daughter and her husband migrated to California, Grandmother followed to be near them and her soon-to-be grandchildren. When Alice's parents later bought a winter home in Palm Desert, California, they reconnected with Mommer and Lew, her husband.

One afternoon while Mommer and Mrs. Joslyn were chatting over tea, Mrs. Joslyn queried, "Jo, where does Marriott go to school? I think Alice needs a better education than we can offer her here."   Referring to where I was currently boarding, Mommer responded, "She goes to Westlake School for Girls."

"We'll check into it. Thanks."

Whenever I visited my grandparents in Palm Springs, the two families arranged a play date where Alice and I could enjoy each other's company. Even though I was a few years older, I enjoyed our time together and swimming in their pool. So when Alice's parents sent her to Westlake as a boarder, I was a familiar face to her since I was boarding also.

Boarding was fun. All the food we wanted to eat, weekend excursions that offered more variety than my usual entertainment of reading a good book, and enjoying the company of a group of girls who were becoming good friends made school more fun than work. Even though we had two hours of required study hall every school night, there was plenty of time for playing tennis, getting into mischief, and taking care of my pet hamster, who died an untimely death from nibbling the chewed gum in the wastebasket where he was confined while I cleaned his cage.

One evening, Alice became ill. Feeling her cheek, I realized she must have a fever. I escorted her to the infirmary where sick girls were isolated to prevent an epidemic. I sympathized with her, and somehow I was allowed to keep her company. To me, she was like the little sister I wish I had. I never considered it a chore when I began putting cold washcloths on her forehead, which was a relief for feverish Alice. During the night we spent together, I refreshed her washcloth whenever it became warm. Alice felt better soon thereafter.

That one act of kindness resulted in a lifelong stream of generosity towards my family and me. While shopping with Alice and Mrs. Joslyn one weekend while I was in high school, she purchased my first two-piece bathing suit. I was thrilled and awed at her generosity.

When I graduated from high school, and later college, she included a generous check in her card. When I announced my engagement to my beloved husband, John, she sent enough money for us to buy a sterling silver set. When each of my seven children were born, she sent a very helpful blessing, enough for a playpen or some other necessary item. When Christmas rolled along, she sent enough to buy a really nice educational gift for all the children to share such as a microscope or the GeoSafari learning set.

After my fourth was born, I felt compelled to ask Mrs. Joslyn if she had ever accepted Jesus as her Savior. She was definitely a good person, but I knew goodness didn't count with God for eternal life. I gently quoted the Bible, "...they have a zeal for God, but not according to knowledge. For they being ignorant of God's righteousness, and seeking to establish their own righteousness, have not submitted to the righteousness of God. For Christ is the end of the law for righteousness to everyone who believes." (Romans 10:2b-4, NKJV) Much to my joy, Mrs. Joslyn confessed her belief in Jesus as her Savior.

When my late husband was murdered, she sent us a very generous gift to buy "something the whole family would enjoy." I purchased a billiard table, where the family still gathers twenty-two years later. Her generous example has inspired me to give sacrificially, sometimes with money if I had it, but more often with time. For example, I helped an acquaintance of my oldest daughters learn to sew. We spent an entire day together, teaching her how to cut a pattern to make the final garment fit her perfectly. She, in turn, sent us Christmas cards for many years until one move too many made us lose touch.

As a reading specialist, I have donated my time to help students learn to read, which gives me a great deal of satisfaction. As a mother, I have volunteered for Missionettes and Pioneer Club, both church youth groups. In addition, the Lord used me to organize neighborhood Bible Clubs, pet shows, 'magic' shows, and drawing classes. I love it when I can help others, share Jesus, and encourage others for which I feel Mrs. Joslyn jump-started me.

Her spirit of generosity has rubbed off on my own children. They give of their time and money to help others also. Two of my sons are selfless rescue workers – one a fire captain and the other a pararescueman. Neighborhood children are drawn like magnets to my unselfish and inclusive daughters' homes. The love of Jesus shining through both daughters have earned them a place as "Aunt" or "Mom" in many children's hearts. Many have accepted Christ as their Lord and Savior as a result.

With much thanks and appreciation to Mrs. Joslyn, who is the inspiration for this chapter, and to the Lord Jesus, who so generously gave His life to save mine.

"But this I say: He who sows sparingly will also reap sparingly,. And he who sows bountifully will also reap bountifully. So let each one give as he purposes in his heart, not grudgingly or of necessity; for God loves a cheerful giver." - 2 Corinthians 9: 6-7, NKJV

Bio:
Marriott Cole was born in Los Angeles, California, graduated from University of Oregon where she accepted Christ as her Savior, and University of West Florida, and currently lives with her husband and two cats near her six children and ten grandchildren.

Blog: www.marriottcole.com
Her Memoir: Grace, Miracles, and Chocolate

#20: Love Covers All Wrongs

By Suzanne Doyle-Ingram

The day Hana was born was the most wonderful day of my life. My husband and I could not believe our good fortune; she was absolutely perfect in every way. We named her Hana because it means 'flower' in Japanese and she was as beautiful as any flower we had ever seen.

After being home from the hospital for a few days, reality starting setting in. Why does she cry so much? Why won't she sleep? Why won't she breast feed? What am I doing wrong? Am I a bad mother? These were the thoughts swirling through my head. Hana was healthy but she had a terrible time breast feeding and she was very colicky. She hardly slept at all, and as a result, neither did I. Truth be told, I was a bit of a mess. I was depressed and I wondered if maybe I should not have had a baby....

When Hana was about 4 weeks old, on the night of September 10, 2001, we were up all night long because she was so fussy. I finally got her to sleep at about 7 in the morning, just as my poor husband was leaving for work (also sleep deprived). I was so grateful for sleep! Hana and I slept until about 10am and it was wonderful to have two precious hours of sleep.

After we got up, I changed her diaper and decided to sit in front of the TV to begin my next 12 hours of breast feeding. I turned on the TV and could not believe what I was seeing. I was completely and utterly shocked. It was September 11, 2001. I had a new baby and the world was coming to an end. At least that's how I felt. How could we have brought a baby into this world where terrorists do such incredibly awful things? I just could not understand it at all. I sat there in front of the TV for hours, tears streaming down my face. I was devastated. I felt like this was a sign from God that I really should not have had a baby. I know that sounds crazy but I was so sleep deprived I didn't even know what I was thinking. I was sadder than I've ever been in my life.

I am Canadian and I lived in Vancouver at that time. I started seeing stories of thousands of travelers being stranded in Eastern Canada because of air travel between the USA and Canada being completely suspended. I was lost at what I could do to help. I thought about donating blood, but then heard that the Blood Donor clinics were completely smashed by thousands of Canadians already doing it.

I felt helpless and alone. I could not get a hold of my husband. By mid-afternoon I knew that I had to get outside to get some fresh air. I decided to get up, get dressed and take Hana out for a walk. While I was out, I stopped in at the local grocery store to pick up a few things for dinner.

I remember so clearly, walking there with Hana facing forward in her little baby carrier strapped to my chest. It was a beautiful sunny day. Everyone we met looked as sad as I felt. But Hana smiled at everyone.

I gathered what I needed for dinner and proceeded to the checkout. The cashier looked nice. I knew my eyes were red and puffy and hoped she wouldn't notice. She rang my items through the scanner one by one and then smiled at me and said, "Because of a random act of kindness, your groceries have all be paid for today."

I couldn't believe it! I wondered what on earth she was talking about. She told me that another customer had come in earlier and said he wanted to buy groceries for someone else as a random act of kindness and she could pick whomever she wanted. And she picked me! I felt happiness spread through my whole body. It wasn't about the money; it was the act of generosity. I felt LOVED. As it says in Proverbs 10:12, "Hatred stirs up dissension, but love covers over all wrongs."

I realized that there are a lot of good people in the world, and that love really can make a difference. By showing my love to others, I know I can make a difference in someone's life as well. Because to the world I might be one person, but to one person I might be the world.

Bio:
Suzanne Doyle-Ingram is a best-selling author who helps people in business write books to attract more of their ideal clients, convert more leads and increase sales revenue.

Suzanne juggles three kids and all their activities with a husband who is an entrepreneur and volunteer firefighter - which keeps the whole family ready to roll at a moment's notice. When not working or driving the kids to all their activities, Suzanne enjoys sunny vacations, good food and cycling on her fancy pink Cruiser.

Connect with Suzanne on Facebook at
http://www.fb.com/SuzanneDoyleIngramBiz or visit her
website for free Book Writing Tips at
http://www.SuzanneDoyleIngram.com.

#21: Giving Honestly and Happily

By Debbie Rivers

"You will be enriched in every way, so that you can be generous on every occasion, and through us your generosity will result in thanksgiving to God." - 2 Corinthians 9:11

Generosity has been the theme of my life's journey for the last year. It did not begin intentionally. It simply began with this thought. I have enough. As the result of a daily gratitude walk and conversations with God, I came to realize the more important truth, He is enough.

Many of us realize that we have more material possessions than most of the world. We know there are people starving and living in less than acceptable conditions, but we don't know how to make our excess, their provision. I will confess - I still don't know how, but I have learned I do not need to travel far to find hunger or substandard living conditions. I can start right where I am.

I never thought my first step would begin just down the street, or would make much of a difference. It was a heart-felt response to a need expressed with humor and camouflaged in levity, but valid and serious, none the less. A friend of our daughter's, was having trouble making ends meet. My daughter delivered a few bags of groceries and returned home wide eyed and sober-minded, to report that her friend really didn't have any food in her home. My partial solution was a simple offering – just one meal – once a week. I left it to my daughter to invite a few other young people, so as not to embarrass or isolate the one who inspired the meal. In just a few short weeks I was feeding ten to fifteen 'twenty-something's every Tuesday night.

What happened next, no one could see coming. First of all, you need to know, I did not publicize this meal. It was not the latest and greatest "outreach" organized by our church. Less than a handful of dear friends knew about what I was doing. So it made it even more incredible when food appeared, seemingly out of nowhere. Supplies showed up. Money was donated. Bags and boxes were left on our front porch. Some weeks they were provisions for the meal itself. Other weeks they were multiples of the same thing so I could send each person home with their own bag of food and goodies. One week my daughter asked me if I knew what I was fixing for dinner or if I was just going to wait until Monday to see what showed up on the front porch. It really was like that. Proverbs 22:9 tells us that the generous will be blessed when we share our food. Every Tuesday night we gathered together with anticipation of that week's 'story' and great thanksgiving for God's truly miraculous provision.

The truth is, we have been blessed so that we can be a blessing. About the same time these meals began, I began hosting Random Acts of Kindness Parties. I have since stopped calling them "random" and instead call them Acts of Kindness Adventures. How and when we step out may seem random, but we quickly recognized God's fingerprints all over these times. Friends and I get together, pool our resources and supplies, and cruise our community to help meet needs and lift spirits. We determined to meet people where they are, put smiles on faces and in some cases, truly be the sudden good break that they need. One thing has led to another. I have now partnered with our local church and our city's Housing Authority to meet the needs of single moms living in public housing in our community. Not a week goes by where I am

73

not called on to meet needs in some way. The requests range from bus passes and birthday presents for children whose parents can't afford them to food, money for utilities, clothing, and furniture.

Because I am just one person, most of the time I need to go to my own wallet, closet or food cupboards first, in order to meet a need. I am amazed at how I can pack up bags of groceries, clothes or linens and hardly feel the loss. There have been times that I have had to give sacrificially, but God is always faithful. Freely, I have received: His provisions, His forgiveness, His mercy and His love. I am continuing to learn that freely, then, I can give the same. I am not an organization with any kind of financial backing. I do, however, know the true Source of every good and perfect gift. Every so often I will get a small check in the mail from a friend or cash slipped into my hand with instructions to use it for whatever needs arise. Inevitably, the timing is just right and it will be just enough. Every time it strengthens my faith.

Scripture tells us that the world will know we are Christians by our love. Many times that must be manifested in tangible ways, not just in words. As a grateful people, blessed by God, we should be at the forefront of giving what we can, when we can, honestly and happily.

"But me – who am I, and who are these my people, that we should presume to be giving something to you? Everything comes from you; all we're doing is giving back what we've been given from your generous hand... It was all yours in the first place! I know, dear God that you care nothing for the surface – You want us, our true selves – and so I have given from the heart, honestly and happily." - 1 Chronicles 29: 14-17 (The Message)

Bio:
Debbie Rivers writes a blog entitled Rivers of Abundance.
You can find it at www.abundantlifestyle.wordpress.com.
She enjoys writing, Acts of Kindness Adventures and seeing
God in everyday moments. Her desire is to encourage others
through her life and her words. Debbie is married and has two
daughters.

Conclusion

By CJ Hitz

Well, you made it through 21 powerful stories of generosity! Even though the book is nearly finished, you can begin writing new stories of generosity from your own life experience. Perhaps you've been inspired to allow God to use your life in generous ways.

It's been my experience that the closer I am to the Lord, the easier His generosity rubs off on me. When I spend intimate time with the Author of generosity, I have a greater desire to be generous with the time, talent, and treasure He's given me. After all, we're blessed to be a blessing. It should be a continuous flow of Him pouring into us and us sharing with others. As 2 Corinthians 9:8 (NLT) says,

"And God will generously provide all you need. Then you will always have everything you need and plenty left over to share with others."

As we read story after story in the New Testament Gospels, we see that people changed after they encountered Jesus. One such encounter involved a tax collector named Zacchaeus who had become very rich. Jesus was passing by and ole' Zac wanted a better look so he climbed a tree nearby (he was a wee little man you know). When Jesus passed that tree, he looked up at Zac and invited himself over for dinner. People grumbled at Jesus hanging out with a "notorious sinner."

But ole' Zac? He was a changed man. Listen to his response to Jesus…

"Zacchaeus stood before the Lord and said, "I will give half my wealth to the poor, Lord, and if I have cheated people on their taxes, I will give them back four times as much!" (Luke 19:8 NLT)

Jesus then responded to Zac…

"Salvation has come to this home today, for this man has shown himself to be a true son of Abraham. For the Son of Man came to seek and save those who are lost." (Luke 19:9-10 NLT)

Jesus rubbed off on this man who made his living by being a crook. Through one encounter over a meal, Zacchaeus went from a hoarder of wealth to a giver of wealth. He simply couldn't give it away fast enough!

And so it is today. When we encounter Jesus on a daily basis, we walk away changed. We also provide others with the opportunity to witness the generosity we receive from the Lord.

Will you choose to allow your life to be used in generous ways? Are you ready for an adventure?

Let the generosity flow!

Get Free Christian Books

Love getting FREE Christian books online? If so, sign up to get notified of new Christian book promotions and never miss out. Then, grab a cup of coffee and enjoy reading the free Christian books you download.

You will also get our FREE report, *"How to Find Free Christian Books Online"* that shows You 9 places you can get new books…for free!

Sign up here:
www.bodyandsoulpublishing.com/freebooks

Happy reading!

Contact Information:

I would love to hear from you! Send me an e-mail to the following address:

cj@cjhitz.com

Websites:
www.bodyandsoulpublishing.com
www.christianspeakers.tv

Fixing our eyes on Jesus,

CJ Hitz

CJ and Shelley Hitz

CJ and Shelley Hitz enjoy sharing God's Truth through their speaking engagements and their writing. On downtime, they enjoy spending time outdoors running, hiking and exploring God's beautiful creation.

To find out more about their ministry check out their website at www.BodyandSoulPublishing.com or to invite them to your next event go to www.ChristianSpeakers.tv.

Note from the Author: Reviews are gold to authors! If you have enjoyed this book, would you consider reviewing it on Amazon.com? Thank you!

Other Books by CJ Hitz

21 Days of Generosity Challenge

Forgiveness Formula

Fuel for the Soul

Unshackled and Free

21 Stories of Gratitude

21 Teen Devotionals...for Guys!

See the entire list here:
www.BodyandSoulPublishing.com/books

Made in the USA
Middletown, DE
15 January 2015